MW00326237

Floral
COCKTAILS

Floral
COCKTAILS

40 fragrant and flavourful flower-powered recipes

Lottie Muir

RYLAND PETERS & SMALL
LONDON • NEW YORK

Designer Emily Breen
Editor Miriam Catley
Head of Production
  Patricia Harrington
Art Director Leslie Harrington
Editorial Director Julia Charles
Publisher Cindy Richards

**All photography by Kim Lightbody
apart from pages**
11 Steve Painter
18 Kate Whitaker
24-25 Emma Mitchell
28 Steve Painter
32 Kate Whitaker
36 Clare Winfield
46 Kate Whitaker
49 & 54 William Reavell
58 Kate Whitaker

Photography © Ryland, Peters & Small
apart from pages 21, 29, 38, 45
(© Kim Lightbody)

First published in 2015 by
CICO Books
This abridged edition published
in 2019 by
Ryland Peters & Small
20–21 Jockey's Fields
London WC1R 4BW
and
341 E 116th St
New York NY 10029
www.rylandpeters.com

Text copyright ©
Lottie Muir 2015, 2019
Design and photographs copyright
© Ryland Peters & Small 2015, 2019

10 9 8 7 6 5 4 3 2 1

Printed and bound in China

ISBN: 978–1–78879-075-8

Note: Foraging wild ingredients requires
expert knowledge and identification. The
photographs and text in this book should
not be used alone for identification
purposes. The author and publisher cannot
be held responsible for, nor shall be liable
for, the erroneous consumption of wild
plants that have caused severe or allergic
reactions resulting from misidentification,
nor the overconsumption of wild plants
that have been shown to be toxic when
consumed in large doses.

All fruit/vegetable/plant/herb ingredients
should be washed before use, particularly
foraged plants.

Sterilizing: Wash bottles and jars, and other
pieces of equipment that need sterilizing,
in very hot, soapy water, then dry them
in an oven set to a low temperature.
Alternatively, you can use some
sterilizing solution/tablets, following the
manufacturer's instructions on the label.

CONTENTS

INTRODUCTION

The recipes in this book encourage you to extend your cocktail cabinet outdoors, using garden and foraged botanical ingredients to infuse and garnish your cocktails. Whether you have a windowsill or a huge garden, this book will hopefully inspire you to make your own delectable cocktail creations.

The explosion of creativity over the last decade in the cocktail scene has created a new Golden Age, which is making the cocktail hour rather longer and more exciting. The return to home-grown, local, and organic ingredients is part of its success. Pioneers from the world of gastronomy, mixology, and, in particular, the slow food movement, have learnt techniques and processes from each other. New rituals and traditions are emerging to create incredible cocktails.

If you factor in the desire to be thrifty as well as decadent, the theme of balance returns. Beauty and thrift, art and science, wholesomeness and revelry— all of them are being used to complement each other. The same is true with the cocktails themselves. Get the strong, weak, bitter, sweet, and sour elements right, and you're pretty much where you need to be.

I've come to cocktails via gardening and foraging. My understanding of cocktails comes from a certain knowledge of plants and a desire to show them off to greatest effect. I have a love of experimenting with alcohol and a desire to enjoy drinking it in as natural a setting as possible. But the idea of wild, floral cocktails is only partly about using foraged ingredients to infuse and garnish your drinks. Hopefully, it also conveys the sense of wildness about the setting in which we, at Midnight Apothecary, serve our cocktails.

I love micro-worlds, whether it's a rock pool, a mossy tree stump, or something in a glass. If they look and smell right, you can lose yourself in them. Their smell alone can conjure up strong emotional responses based on memory; for example, a summer's day or a walk in a wood. At their best, cocktails—and gardens —are magical creations that balance wildness and design in an orgy of the senses.

Our recipe at Midnight Apothecary is really very simple. Take one patch of ground. Scatter liberally with seeds and love. Harvest the bounty, stick it in a glass, light a fire, and invite the people. They will come and they will love it!

Botanical Bar

THE SOUR AND THE STRONG

Whether it's the honey notes of false acacia-infused gin, the subtle, delicious floral rose petal vodka, or the bold, peppery flavor of nasturtium rum, using foraged, natural treasures in your cocktail cabinet will make your cocktails look, smell, feel, and taste wonderful.

RASPBERRY AND SCENTED GERANIUM SHRUB

All you need for this recipe, apart from your ingredients, is a tiny bit of patience and a spare surface in your kitchen to let the macerating fruit and leaves do their magic with the sugar.

18 oz (500 g) very ripe raspberries, washed

10 scented geranium (*Pelargonium*) leaves

4 cups (800 g) superfine (caster) sugar

approx. 2 cups (500 ml) champagne vinegar or apple cider vinegar

sealable presentation bottle(s), sterilized

Makes approx. 1 pint (500 ml)

Place the raspberries in a large bowl. Smack the unwashed scented geranium leaves between your palms to release the essential oils, and place them among the raspberries. Cover them with the sugar. Drape a clean dishtowel over the top of the bowl and leave on a countertop.

The maceration will take up to 48 hours—you will notice the sugar turn red, and under the crust an amazing bright raspberry liquid will appear. Strain the liquid into a measuring cup. Add an equal amount of champagne vinegar or apple cider vinegar to the amount of liquid in the measuring cup. Stir to make sure all the sugar in the liquid has dissolved. Funnel into the sterilized presentation bottle(s) and seal. This shrub will mellow with time, so try to leave it for a week before consuming. Store in the refrigerator once opened and consume within 6 months.

CRAB APPLE VERJUICE

Crab apples, the unpromising fruits of *Malus sylvestris*, found in hedgerows as well as on street corners, yield a beautiful syrup and are the perfect acidifying agent for some foraged cocktails, like the Hedgerow Sour (page 53). It's their very sourness, which makes crab apples so inedible raw, that is the clue to their success—they are packed with malic acid, which can be used in place of citric acid to make verjuice. Crab Apple Verjuice contains only half the acidity of lemon juice and is much sweeter, so you do need to use it carefully.

2¼ pounds (1kg) crab apples (ripe enough so their seeds are black)

enough water to cover the crab apples

1 tbsp vodka, 80 proof/40% ABV (optional)

food processor or blender
several layers of cheesecloth (muslin) or a jelly bag with weights or an apple press or potato ricer
sealable presentation bottle, sterilized

Makes approx. 1½ cups (355 ml)

Wash the apples but do not cut them. Pour enough water into a large, nonreactive pan to cover the apples and bring to a rolling boil. Add the apples whole, bring back to a boil, and blanch for 1 minute—this makes the fruit softer and easier to press. Remove from the heat and run under cold water.

Add the crab apples in batches to the food processor or blender and blitz them to a pulp. If they are particularly large apples, you may need to halve them. Strain the pulped mix into a large, wide-mouthed pitcher (jug) through a fine-mesh sieve lined with several layers of cheesecloth (muslin) or a jelly bag, and weighed down with something heavy (like cans of food) to extract the juice. Alternatively, use an apple press or a potato ricer.

Funnel the juice into the sterilized presentation bottle and seal, adding 1 tablespoon of high-proof alcohol if you want to preserve the verjuice. If you don't add any alcohol, the sugars and yeast are likely to ferment. It is OK to let this happen over a couple of days (some people prefer to do this anyway) and then add the alcohol to stop the fermentation process. Store in a cool, dark place for up to a year. Once opened, use within a month.

SCENTED GERANIUM VODKA

Scented geraniums (*Pelargonium*) are a fantastic aromatic and visual addition to gardens and cocktails. The leaves can be rubbed and sniffed as an appetite-stimulating garnish on a foam, or the leaves can be infused in a spirit or syrup. The flowers make an attractive garnish, with a faint citrus flavor.

2 large handfuls of unsprayed rose-scented geranium leaves, such as *Pelargonium graveolens* or *P.* 'Attar of Roses'

700 or 750 ml bottle of vodka, 80 proof/40% ABV

1-quart (1-liter) wide-mouthed, sealable jar, sterilized
sealable presentation bottle(s), sterilized

Makes approx. 1 ½ pints (750 ml)

Smack the individual unwashed leaves between your hands to release the essential oil before dropping them into the jar. Cover with the vodka. Seal and upend the jar gently a couple of times. Leave in a cool, dark place for 24 hours.

Taste to see if you are getting a strong flavor of scented geranium. If you aren't, reseal and leave for a maximum of 48 hours. Strain the infusion into a wide-mouthed pitcher (jug), then funnel into the sterilized presentation bottle(s) and seal. Store in a cool, dark place and use within 6 months.

LAVENDER GIN

English lavender (*Lavandula angustifolia*) is the most fragrant and, therefore, the perfect type of lavender for this recipe. I like the cultivar 'Munstead'. *L. × intermedia* 'Provence' (French lavender) has a milder, sweeter flavor, which is also good. Lavender is particularly potent, so use it sparingly, and only infuse it for a very short time, otherwise a nasty bitterness will pervade. Get the balance right and you'll have floral notes singing beautifully in a wide variety of summer cocktails.

6 tsp fresh lavender blossoms or 2 tsp dried, fragrant, culinary-grade lavender

1 liter bottle of floral gin, such as Jensen Old Tom

1-quart (1-liter) wide-mouthed, sealable jar, sterilized
sealable presentation bottle(s), sterilized

Makes approx. 1 quart (1 liter)

Place the fresh or dried lavender blossoms in the jar. Pour in the gin. Seal the jar, upend it gently a couple of times, and place somewhere dark at room temperature. Leave for 5–8 hours, testing after 5 hours, then every hour to

make sure there is no bitterness emerging. (To speed things up, heat the lavender gently in a pan with half the gin. As soon as it reaches boiling point, take off the heat, let cool, and add the remaining gin.) Strain the infusion into the sterilized presentation bottle(s), seal, and store in a cool, dark place. Both methods will result in a gin with a pinkish-purple hue.

FALSE ACACIA GIN

I have three huge false acacia or black locust (*Robinia pseudoacacia*) trees on the terrace outside Midnight Apothecary. In late spring, they are laden with huge heads of fragrant, white blossoms. I simply infuse them in gin and use in Martinis to provide honey notes without the cloying sweetness.

6 heads of false acacia blossoms
1 liter bottle of gin, 80 proof/ 40% ABV

1-quart (1-liter) wide-mouthed, sealable jar, sterilized
sealable presentation bottle(s), sterilized

Makes approx. 1 quart (1 liter)

Shake the blossom heads free of wildlife and cut off any stems or greenery. Place the individual unwashed blossoms in the jar and pour over the gin. Seal, shake gently, and keep in a cool, dark place. Taste after the second day—I usually find the infusion is ready after about 4 days. Strain the infusion into a wide-mouthed pitcher (jug), then funnel into the sterilized presentation bottle(s) and seal. Store in a cool, dark place and consume within 6 months.

ROSE PETAL VODKA

This infusion is quite subtle and delicious. I took a tip from Liz Knight of Forage Fine Foods in Herefordshire, U.K., who makes the most exquisite rose petal syrup. She snips off the bitter white bits at the bottom of each petal. I also only pick the petals, rather than the central flower, as I want to be able to come back later in the year to pick the rosehips.

enough rose petals to fill the jar loosely
700 or 750 ml bottle of vodka, 80 proof/40% ABV
2 tbsp (25g) superfine (caster) sugar, to taste

1-quart (1-liter) wide-mouthed, sealable jar, sterilized
sealable presentation bottle(s), sterilized

Makes approx. 1½ pints (750 ml)

Pick over the rose petals to remove any wildlife, but do not wash them. Loosely pack them into the jar. Pour the vodka up to the very top of the jar to ensure there is no air. Leave for 24 hours and taste—it will be ready when there is an earthy, pungent scent of roses. The taste deteriorates after the third day, so check regularly.

Strain the infusion into a wide-mouthed pitcher (jug). Clean and dry the jar. Pour the infusion back into it. Add sugar to taste. It's better to err on the less sweet side, as you can always add a sweetener to your cocktails later. Once ready, use a funnel to pour into the sterilized presentation bottle(s) and seal. Store in a cool, dark place and use within 6 months.

ROSE PETAL GIN

Gin makes a delicious alternative to vodka, but I would urge you to use a gin that contains only a few botanicals to reduce the chance of your rose petals clashing with other flavors.

NASTURTIUM RUM

Many flowers look fantastic but taste insipid. However, nasturtiums are bold in appearance as well as flavor. The sweetness of the molasses or sugarcane juice in rum needs a punchy, spicy flavor to team up with, and the pepperiness of nasturtium is ideal. Once your infusion is ready, a fresh nasturtium flower will look stunning in the finished cocktail and, if you eat the whole blossom, you'll get the sweetness of the nectar alongside the spiciness of the pepper. The leaves are also deliciously peppery.

enough nasturtium flowers (about 40) to fill the jar loosely

1 liter bottle of golden rum, 80 proof/40% ABV

1-quart (1-liter) wide-mouthed, sealable jar, sterilized

sealable presentation bottle(s), sterilized

Makes approx. 1 ½ pints (750ml)

Pick over the nasturtium flowers and remove any wildlife. Pack the unwashed blossoms gently into the jar and pour the rum over the top, making sure the flowers are completely covered. Seal the jar, upend it gently a couple of times, and leave in a cool, dark place. The pepperiness takes a while to really work in this infusion, so check after 7 days and wait a maximum of 3 weeks—certainly no longer. Strain the infusion into a wide-mouthed pitcher (jug), then funnel into the sterilized presentation bottle(s) and seal. Store in a cool, dark place and consume within 6 months.

OTHER NASTURTIUM INFUSIONS

Use tequila, gin, or vodka in place of the rum.

THE SWEET

Most cocktails need a sweetener to balance out the acidity and bitterness, but moderation is the key. Over-sweetened cocktails create a sickly mouth feel and can mask other flavors. When you are using fantastic base spirits and natural ingredients, there is far less need for sugar. Fresh fruits provide their own, and there are some plants that can be employed to create the desired levels of sweetness.

SIMPLE SYRUP

Many recipes will call for simple syrup, which is simply 1:1 sugar to water. White superfine (caster) sugar works well when you want a brighter, clearer syrup.

1 part superfine (caster) sugar to 1 part water

Heat the sugar and water on a low heat and stir until the sugar is thoroughly dissolved. Add a tablespoon of 80 proof/40% ABV vodka to increase the syrup's shelf life. Once cooled, funnel into a sterilized bottle and store in the refrigerator for up to 2 weeks—up to a month if you have added vodka.

You can omit the heating process and simply combine equal amounts of sugar and water in a bottle or jar, then seal and shake vigorously until the sugar is dissolved, but the syrup won't be quite as thick.

HONEY SIMPLE SYRUP

Honey is a fantastic ingredient, both for the flavor of the flowers, on which the bees have been gorging, and for its health-giving properties. It is too thick to use on its own, so simply combine equal parts honey and water, and heat until the honey is thoroughly dissolved to give a delicious floral simple syrup.

WILD HIBISCUS SYRUP

Add equal volumes of dried flowers, sugar, and water—for example, 1 cup of flowers, 1 cup of superfine (caster) sugar, 1 cup of water—to a nonreactive pan and bring to a boil. Remove from the heat and let the ingredients steep for 20 minutes. Strain, reserving the calyx (flowers) as a garnish.

ROSEMARY SYRUP

Add equal volumes of sugar and water to a nonreactive pan and bring to a boil. Let simmer until clear and slightly thickened. Take off the heat and add 3 sprigs of rosemary. When cool, strain into a sterilized bottle. Store in the refrigerator for up to 3 weeks.

GINGER SYRUP

This syrup will come in handy, not just for your cocktails, but also for a variety of gastronomic delights like marinades and desserts.

2 cups (400 g) superfine (caster) sugar

2 cups (500 ml) water

2½ oz (75 g) fresh ginger, fairly thickly sliced

1 tbsp lemon juice or 80 proof/ 40% ABV vodka (optional)

sealable presentation bottle(s), sterilized

Makes approx. 1 pint (500 ml)

Place the sugar and water in a nonreactive pan and slowly bring to a boil. Add the ginger and let simmer for 5 minutes. Remove from the heat and let the ginger steep for another 10 minutes.

Strain the syrup into a wide-mouthed pitcher (jug) and then funnel into the sterilized presentation bottle(s) and seal. Store in the refrigerator and consume within 2 weeks. A tablespoon of lemon juice or high-proof vodka added just after removing the pan from the heat will increase the shelf life of the syrup for up to a month.

HONEYSUCKLE SYRUP

Wild honeysuckle (*Lonicera periclymenum*) is a heady feast for the senses. *Lonicera japonica* is equally sweet and delicious and, like wild honeysuckle, can be found naturalized across Europe and North America, scrambling over gardens, walls, and wasteland. There is debate about the toxicity of certain species of honeysuckle (and their berries in particular) so stick to these two species and avoid the berries. Honeysuckle has the strongest scent at night, so try to harvest unopened or newly opened flowers during the evening or early morning.

8 large handfuls of unsprayed honeysuckle flowers, leaves and stems removed

approx. 2 cups (400 g) superfine (caster) sugar

juice of ½ lemon

sealable presentation bottle(s), sterilized

Makes approx. 1 pint (500 ml)

Place the honeysuckle flowers in a nonreactive bowl and cover with cold water, then leave to steep for 12 hours, or at least overnight, at room temperature. Make sure the flowers are completely covered by the water.

Strain the mixture into a measuring cup, discarding the flowers. Pour the liquid into a nonreactive pan. Measure an equal amount of sugar to the liquid and add to the pan. Bring to a boil, and let simmer for 5 minutes. Feel free to replace half the sugar with a handful of chopped sweet cicely leaves, but bear in mind that this will adjust the color.

Remove from the heat, let cool, add the lemon juice, and funnel into the sterilized presentation bottle(s).

WILD VIOLET SYRUP

Although this very sweet and floral syrup is a fiddle to make because the wild violet (*Viola odorata*) flowers are tiny and you need a lot of them, and the petals also have to be removed individually from their stems and flower centers, it really is worth it.

7 large handfuls of wild violet petals, stems and flower centers removed

2 cups (500 ml) boiling water

approx. 2 cups (400 g) granulated sugar

1 tbsp lemon juice (optional)

1 tbsp vodka (optional)

1-quart (1-liter) wide-mouthed, sealable jar, sterilized
sealable presentation bottle(s), sterilized

Makes approx. 1 pint (500 ml)

Place the petals in the jar, pour the boiling water over them, and seal. Let the petals infuse for 12 hours.

Strain the liquid into a measuring cup, then pour into a nonreactive pan. For every cup of liquid, add 1 cup (200 g) sugar. Heat gently until the sugar has dissolved (make sure it does not boil, or the blue color will take on a gray tinge). Once cooled, funnel into the sterilized presentation bottle(s) and seal. If you are not happy with the color, use a dropper or pipette to add lemon juice, drop by drop, until it is the perfect shade of violet. (If desired, add a tablespoon of vodka to make the syrup last longer.) Seal and store in the refrigerator. Use within 3 months.

GORSE FLOWER SYRUP

You will find carpets of gorse (*Ulex europaeus*) by the coast, on heathland, in town parks, and on wasteland. The pain of harvesting the beautiful acid-yellow flowers from this extremely dense, spiny shrub is worth it for the coconut and almond-tasting syrup.

4 large handfuls of gorse flowers

2 cups (400 g) superfine (caster) sugar

4 cups (1 liter) water

juice of ½ lemon

zest of ½ unwaxed, organic orange, without any white pith

sealable presentation bottle(s), sterilized

Makes approx. 1 quart (1 liter)

De-bug the gorse flowers and remove any greenery or spines. Combine the sugar and water in a pan until the solution reaches boiling point. Take off the heat and immediately add the unwashed flowers, lemon juice, and orange zest. Let cool.

Strain the liquid into a wide-mouthed pitcher (jug), then funnel into the sterilized presentation bottle(s) and seal immediately. The syrup will keep for up to 1 month in the refrigerator.

ROSE PETAL SYRUP

This recipe involves massage, roses, and perfume… don't blame me if things get out of hand! Use the most perfumed roses you can find, and make sure they are unsprayed. It also helps if their petals are quite thin. Two good choices that grow wild and adorn many a private and public space are *Rosa rugosa* and the wild dog rose, *R. canina*. Whenever I use wild dog rose, which has very delicate pink petals, I add a few petals of a red rose to give a really rich-colored syrup.

6 handfuls of pink and/or red rose petals

6 cups (1.2 kg) superfine (caster) sugar

3 cups (750 ml) water

zest of ½ unwaxed, organic orange

1 tbsp lemon juice

pinch of salt

sealable presentation bottle(s), sterilized

Makes approx. 1½ pints (750 ml)

Snip off the bitter white tip at the base of each petal—it's a little awkward to do but worth it. Alternatively, when picking the petals from the rosebush, pull the petals in a clump with one hand and snip the base off in one go with the other.

Loosely pack the petals in a nonreactive bowl and add about 2 cups (400 g) of the sugar. Gently massage the sugar into the petals to bruise them and start the maceration. Cover with a clean dishtowel and leave overnight or for up to 12 hours.

You should return to a gooey mess, where the petals have shrunk and the sugar has extracted some color and flavor out of them. Tip this sugar and petal mix into a nonreactive pan, add the remaining sugar, the water, orange zest, lemon juice, and a pinch of salt, and gently bring to a boil. You will notice that the color transfers from the petals into the liquid. Let simmer for 5 minutes or until you have a thick, unctuous syrup.

Let the syrup cool. Strain it into a wide-mouthed pitcher, then funnel into the sterilized presentation bottle(s) and seal. You can store the syrup in the refrigerator for well over a month.

ROSEHIP SYRUP

At Midnight Apothecary, we use hedgerow syrups like this in colorful autumnal cocktails, such as Berried Treasure, where jewels of concentrated fruit flavor burst in your mouth in an otherwise grown-up cocktail. They also work very well in Sours, where lemon juice and egg white balance the sweetness. The huge hips of the Japanese rose (*Rosa rugosa*) are excellent for this completely delicious syrup, as their large size means less chopping.

2¼ pounds (1 kg) rosehips
about 3 quarts (3 liters) water
5 cups (1 kg) superfine (caster) sugar
juice of ½ lemon or 1 tbsp vodka
sealable presentation bottle(s), sterilized

Makes approx. 1 quart (1 liter)

Wash and chop the rosehips in half. Bring 1½ quarts (1.5 liters) of the water to a boil in a large, nonreactive pan. Add the rosehips. Return to a boil, simmer for 5 minutes, and remove from the heat. Let cool slightly.

Strain the rosehip mixture carefully through a jelly bag or layers of cheesecloth (muslin) suspended above a large bowl. Put the pulp back in the cleaned pan with the remaining 1½ quarts (1.5 liters) of water, bring to a boil, remove from the heat, and strain again as above.

Combine the juice from both strains with the sugar and bring to a boil. Boil hard for at least 10 minutes or until you get a thick, syrupy consistency. Remove from the heat and add the lemon juice or vodka. Funnel into the sterilized presentation bottle(s) and seal.

LILAC SYRUP

The humble fragrant lilac (*Syringa vulgaris*) makes a delightful syrup. If its color turns out a bit insipid, add a couple of mahonia berries, blackberries, or blueberries to darken it.

2 cups (about 6 heads) lilac blossoms
1 cup (200 g) superfine (caster) sugar
1 cup (250 ml) water
zest of ½ unwaxed, organic orange
1 tbsp lemon juice
sealable presentation bottle(s), sterilized

Makes approx. 1½ pints (750 ml)

De-bug the blossoms and remove them from the green bitter stems.

Place the sugar and water in a nonreactive pan and stir over a low heat until it boils. Add the unwashed lilac blossoms and orange zest, and bring back to a boil. Simmer for 10 minutes. Add the lemon juice. Strain the liquid into a wide-mouthed pitcher (jug) while still piping hot, then funnel into the sterilized presentation bottle(s) and seal. Store in the refrigerator and use within 1 month.

CRAB APPLE SYRUP

This beautiful, orangey-pink, floral-scented syrup could not be further removed from the jaw-clenching sourness of an uncooked crab apple. The recipe requires patience: the juice has to drip, drop by drop, through a very fine strainer or several layers of cheesecloth, otherwise it will turn cloudy.

3¼ pounds (1.5 kg) crab apples
3½ cups (700 g) superfine (caster) sugar
juice of ½ lemon

sealable presentation bottle(s), sterilized

Makes approx. 1 quart (1 liter)

Wash the crab apples and remove any stems, greenery, and blossom ends. If the apples are golf-ball size or bigger, cut them in half. Place in a nonreactive pan and pour in just enough water to cover. Bring to a boil and let simmer until the apples are soft (about 25 minutes). Strain the pulp carefully through a jelly bag or several layers of cheesecloth suspended above a large bowl or pan. Let the pulp move through the filter very slowly.

Measure your final amount of juice—for every 1 quart (1 liter), add 3½ cups (700 g) sugar. Add the juice and sugar to the cleaned pan and bring to a boil. Then add the lemon juice and boil hard for about 10 minutes until you have a syrup consistency. Skim off any froth. Funnel the syrup into the sterilized presentation bottle(s) and seal. Store in a cool, dark place. Once opened, use within a month.

YARROW SYRUP

The flowers of yarrow (*Achillea millefolium*) are bitter and astringent, but when sweetened, they make a beautiful syrup. Delicate, with an almost lavender taste, the syrup works very well with tequila. [Please note that yarrow contains trace amounts of thujone which is a uterine stimulant, so should be avoided during pregnancy.]

2 tbsp yarrow flowers
2 cups (500 ml) boiling water
1¼ cups (425 g) agave nectar (or honey)
1½ cups (355 ml) water

sealable presentation bottle(s), sterilized

Makes approx. ¾ pint (375 ml)

Remove any wildlife and stalks from the flower heads. Place in a nonreactive pan. Pour the boiling water over the flowers and steep for 15 minutes. Strain the liquid into a wide-mouthed pitcher.

Return this "tea" to the cleaned pan and add the agave nectar (or honey) and 1½ cups (355 ml) water. Bring to a boil and let simmer for a couple of minutes. Remove from the heat for 15 minutes before funneling into the sterilized presentation bottle(s). Seal and store in the refrigerator and use within a couple of months.

MEADOWSWEET SYRUP

Soft clouds of creamy, fluffy meadowsweet (*Filipendula ulmaria*) blossom appear on Walthamstow Marshes in east London, close to Midnight Apothecary, during early and mid-summer. Interspersed with pink and purple wild vetches and peas, they are a beautiful sight, and the heady, almond, vanilla, and honey scent is easily transferred to an exquisite syrup, which I actually prefer to elderflower cordial.

15 heads of meadowsweet blossoms, fully opened
5 cups (1 kg) superfine (caster) sugar
1 quart (1 liter) water
zest and juice of 1 unwaxed, organic lemon
sealable presentation bottle(s), sterilized

Makes approx. 1 quart (1 liter)

Strip the meadowsweet blossoms from the stems, and put to one side to give the wildlife plenty of time to evacuate.

Make a simple syrup by heating the sugar and water in a nonreactive pan over a low heat, stirring to dissolve the sugar. Once it reaches boiling point, remove the pan from the heat. Add the lemon zest and flowers. Submerge the flowers in the syrup, cover, and leave overnight or for up to 12 hours, to infuse.

Add the lemon juice, stir, then strain into a wide-mouthed pitcher (jug) to remove the flowers and lemon zest.

Reheat the syrup gently in a clean nonreactive pan and funnel into the sterilized presentation bottle(s) while piping hot and seal. Store somewhere cool and dark. Once opened, keep in the refrigerator for 2–3 months.

RHUBARB SYRUP

This is a fantastic-looking as well as tasting syrup, especially if you find really red rhubarb stalks. Sweet cicely grows and works perfectly with rhubarb as a sweetener. If you don't have any, just omit and double the amount of sugar.

4 cups (700 g) bright red rhubarb, cut into 1-in (2.5-cm) slices
1 cup (200 g) superfine (caster) sugar
4 tbsp (10 g) finely chopped sweet cicely (*Myrrhis odorata*) leaves
2 cups (500 ml) water
1–2 thin slices of fresh ginger (optional)
1 tbsp vodka (optional)
sealable presentation bottle(s), sterilized

Makes approx. 1½ pints (750 ml)

Put all main ingredients in a nonreactive pan and bring to a boil over a medium heat. Let simmer until the rhubarb disintegrates and becomes pulpy (about 15–20 minutes). While the liquid is still piping hot, strain into a wide-mouthed pitcher (jug), then funnel into the sterilized presentation bottle(s) and seal. Store in the refrigerator and use within 2 weeks. Add a tablespoon of vodka to make it last longer.

LEMON VERBENA AND RASPBERRY SYRUP

Lemon verbena (*Aloysia citrodora*) is just about my favorite herb. It's nothing to look at, but the smell and taste of those little leaves pack such a lemony, aromatic, sweet punch. You don't need many of them to get fantastic results. It's a natural bedfellow for raspberries, and this syrup forms the sweet component in the Raspberry and Scented Geranium Sour (page 42).

2 cups (500 ml) water

2 cups (400 g) superfine (caster) sugar (you could substitute half the sugar with 2 tbsp/5 g or 2 young stems of sweet cicely (*Myrrhis odorata*) leaves, finely chopped, for a slight aniseed flavor)

1 cup (125 g) raspberries

4 lemon verbena leaves

sealable presentation bottle(s), sterilized

Makes approx. 1 pint (500 ml)

Stir the water and sugar together in a nonreactive pan over a low heat to make a simple syrup. Once it has reached boiling point, add the raspberries and lemon verbena leaves, stir, and let simmer until the raspberries have collapsed (about 10 minutes).

Strain while still piping hot, but not boiling, into a wide-mouthed pitcher (jug)—you really don't want raspberry pips in this syrup —then funnel into the sterilized presentation bottle(s).

Seal and store in the refrigerator for up to 2 weeks. The remaining raspberry pulp (with lemon verbena solids removed) can be used as a compote over yogurt or ice cream.

LEMON BALM LIQUEUR

The sweet, citrussy flavor of lemon balm (*Melissa officinalis*) makes this herb a great ingredient in many cocktails, such as the Lemon Balm and Nasturtium Daisy (page 44). If you can find a cultivar of lemon balm called *M. officinalis* 'Quedlinburger Niederliegende', go for it, because it has a very high concentration of essential oils and therefore fragrance.

3 cups (100 g) organic lemon balm leaves

zest of 3 unwaxed, organic lemons

1 liter bottle of vodka, 80 proof/ 40% ABV

1 cup (200 g) superfine (caster) sugar (optional)

1-quart (1-liter) wide-mouthed, sealable jar, sterilized
sealable presentation bottle(s), sterilized

Makes approx. 1 quart (1 liter)

Gently wash and dry the lemon balm leaves. Slap them between your hands to release the essential oils, then place in the sterilized jar. Add the lemon zest, vodka, and sugar. Seal the jar and upend it gently a couple of times. Store in a cool, dark place for a month, turning it every other day.

Strain the liquid into a wide-mouthed pitcher (jug). Taste. If you prefer a sweeter liqueur, make a simple syrup by heating equal parts of superfine (caster) sugar and water, let it cool, and add to the liqueur until you have the desired level of sweetness. Funnel into the sterilized presentation bottle(s) and seal. This is another liqueur that is great to store in the freezer. Use within a year.

ELDERFLOWER LIQUEUR

Another case of cocktail alchemy, the common, workhorse shrub elderberry (*Sambucus nigra*), which grows in towns and rural areas alike, produces a variety of almost year-round ingredients. The elderflowers signal the start of summer and produce a floral, elegant liqueur.

20 large elderflower heads
½ cup (100 g) superfine (caster) sugar
1 liter bottle of vodka, 80 proof/ 40% ABV
1 unwaxed, organic lemon, thinly sliced

1-quart (1-liter) wide-mouthed, sealable jar, sterilized
sealable presentation bottle(s), sterilized

Makes approx. 1 quart (1 liter)

Shake the elderflower heads free of unwanted wildlife but do not wash them. Remove all the leaves and as many stalks as you can, as these are slightly toxic (the very tiny stalks that are attached to each flower are fine).

Place the flowers in the sterilized jar and compress slightly with your hand. Add the sugar, followed by the vodka —adding the sugar at this stage draws out the flavor of the elderflowers. Place the lemon slices on top of the flowers to weigh them down—you don't want the flowers to oxidize by rising above the surface of the alcohol. If the lemon slices don't do the trick, add a small plate or a lid that fits snugly in the jar.

Seal the jar and store in a cool, dark place for a month. Upend it gently a couple of times during the month, to make sure the sugar has dissolved. After 1 month, strain the liquid twice into a wide-mouthed pitcher (jug), first through a fine-mesh strainer to remove the flower debris, then through a coffee filter or several layers of cheesecloth (muslin) so that the liqueur is not cloudy. Funnel into the sterilized presentation bottle(s) and seal. Store somewhere cool and dark. Once opened, keep in the refrigerator and consume within 6 months.

GARNISHES

Garnishes are there not just to look pretty; they should provide integral, complementary flavors, aromas, and textures.

Candied Cherry Blossom Make about ⅓ cup (75 ml) of egg wash by mixing 1 lightly whisked egg white and ½ cup (100 g) superfine (caster) sugar. Using a fine paintbrush, paint each individual petal on both sides with a light coating of the egg wash and, with your fingers, scatter a light coating of sugar over them before placing on a sheet of parchment paper inside a tray on a sunny windowsill or in a warm area. They may take 24–48 hours to dry. Once dried, store in an airtight container and use within a week.

Candied Rosehips Add about ⅔ cup (130 g) superfine (caster) sugar, ¼ cup (60 ml) water, and 1 cup (250 g) rosehips (halved, with their hairy, pithy seeds and membrane removed) into a nonreactive pan. Heat over a medium-high heat until it is boiling vigorously. Tip the rosehips into the pan to coat them and then transfer them to parchment paper sprinkled with superfine (caster) sugar. Coat them in sugar and let cool. Once dry, store in an airtight container and use within 2 weeks.

Citrus Spiral To make lemon spirals (also, confusingly, sometimes called twists), cut the ends of the lemon and make an incision halfway through the lemon lengthwise. Use your thumb to separate the rind from the meat of the lemon until you have removed the whole skin. Roll up the whole skin (including the pith) and cut in pieces to make long, curly twists. Secure the rolls of twists with toothpicks (cocktail sticks) until you need to use them.

Citrus Twist A lemon twist, or zest, is an elongated, oval-shaped slice of lemon that you peel off with a vegetable peeler or paring knife. Squeeze the zest over the cocktail, skin side down, to release the essential oils. You can set fire to the oil by holding a match in one hand and zest in the other. Finish by wiping the zest around the rim of the glass and dropping in the drink, to add a wonderful flavor and aroma.

Drying Herbs To dry soft herbs swiftly, place the freshly picked herbs in a single layer on a baking sheet. Place in an oven heated to the lowest possible setting until the herbs are brittle or crumble easily.

The
Cocktails

PRETTY IN PINK

This cocktail is a take on the classic Ramos Gin Fizz. I use rose-petal infused gin and rose water (you can buy bottles in supermarkets or Middle Eastern stores) in place of orange flower water, and I add a little Rose Petal Syrup with the rhubarb syrup to provide extra floral notes to this baby-pink, creamy drink. It's divine.

2 oz (60 ml) Rose Petal Gin (page 14)

dash of rose water

½ oz (15 ml) heavy (double) cream

½ oz (15 ml) freshly squeezed lemon juice

½ oz (15 ml) freshly squeezed lime juice

½ oz (15 ml) Rhubarb Syrup (page 22)

1 tsp (5 ml) Rose Petal Syrup (page 18)

1 large egg white

1 oz (30 ml) soda water

rosebud or petal, to garnish

Combine all the ingredients (except the ice, soda water, and rose garnish) in a cocktail shaker. Cover and shake hard for at least 25 seconds to really emulsify the egg and marry the different consistencies thoroughly. Fill the shaker two-thirds of the way up with ice. Cover again and shake hard for at least another 20 seconds. Strain the mixture into the glass. Pour the soda water into the shaker to loosen any remaining froth, then gently pour into the glass to form extra foam on top of the cocktail. Garnish with a rosebud or rose petal.

LAVENDER BEE'S KNEES

This is a take on a classic Prohibition-era cocktail of gin, honey, and lemon juice. Initially, it was created to mask the dubious quality of the liquor of the day. This version brings the glorious lavender-infused gin to the fore, with the honey and lavender working extremely well together.

2 oz (60 ml) Lavender Gin (page 11)
¾ oz (20 ml) Honey Simple Syrup (page 15)
½ oz (15 ml) freshly squeezed lemon juice
lavender sprig, to garnish

Add all the ingredients (except the lavender garnish) to a cocktail shaker and fill it two-thirds of the way up with ice. Cover and shake hard for 20 seconds, then strain the contents of the shaker into a cocktail glass. Garnish with the sprig of lavender.

CHELSEA FRINGE COLLINS

I was asked to design a cocktail for The Chelsea Fringe, the alternative to the more famous Chelsea Flower Show—the annual spectacle of English eccentricity, passion, and obsession with plants and gardening. My Chelsea Fringe Collins was designed to look, taste, and smell like "summer in a glass."

2 oz (60 ml) jasmine-infused Jensen Old Tom Gin
½ oz (15 ml) Elderflower Liqueur (page 24)
½ oz (15 ml) Rose Petal Syrup (page 18)
dash of orange bitters
¾ oz (20 ml) freshly squeezed lemon juice
soda water
dash of cassis (optional)
wild strawberries, wild fennel fronds, lavender sprig,
borage flowers, dianthus petals, lemon twist, to garnish

Fill a collins glass with ice. Tuck some wild strawberries, fennel fronds, the lavender sprig, borage flowers, and a few dianthus petals in among the ice cubes, sandwiched against the glass, for maximum visual impact. Save a few borage flowers for the final garnish. Add the gin, Elderflower Liqueur, Rose Petal Syrup, orange bitters, and lemon juice to a cocktail shaker. Fill it two-thirds full with ice, cover, and shake hard for 20 seconds. Strain the mixture into the chilled glass over the ice.

Garnish with the lemon twist and remaining borage flowers, using the tweezers or small tongs, then top with the soda water. Use a pipette or the top of a barspoon to drop the cassis to the bottom of the glass to create a color contrast (optional).

LAVENDER GIN FIZZ

Lavender adds a subtle, floral note to summer drinks. It combines particularly well with honey, citrus, and bitter flavors. I add a dash of Parfait Amour (a dark purple liqueur, flavored with rose and violet petals, vanilla beans/pods, and orange blossom) simply to intensify the lavender color.

2 oz (60 ml) Lavender Gin (page 11)
¾ oz (20 ml) Honey Simple Syrup (page 15)
¾ oz (20 ml) freshly squeezed lemon juice
dash of Parfait Amour
dash of orange bitters
soda water
lavender sprig, to garnish

Fill a collins glass with ice. Add all the ingredients, except the soda water and lavender garnish, to a cocktail shaker and fill it two-thirds full with ice. Cover and shake hard for 20 seconds. Strain the mixture into the chilled glass over the ice. Cut a sprig of lavender to fit just above the rim of the glass. Top with soda water. Add a straw and serve.

HIBISCUS AND BLACKCURRANT LEAF MOJITO

The beautiful flowers of blackcurrant sage and blackcurrant leaves in the Midnight Apothecary garden in mid-summer provided the inspiration for this cocktail.

I lime, cut into 6 wedges
5 small blackcurrant leaves, 3 whole and 2 finely sliced
I tsp (5 ml) turbinado (demerara) sugar
¾ oz (20 ml) Wild Hibiscus Syrup (page 15)
2 oz (60 ml) spiced rum
soda water
sprig of blackcurrant sage in flower, blackcurrant leaves,
and hollyhock (*Alcea*) flower, to garnish

Put 4 wedges of lime, 3 whole blackcurrant leaves, and the sugar in a collins glass, and muddle. Add the Wild Hibiscus Syrup. Half-fill the glass with ice. Add the rum, the remaining 2 lime wedges, and the 2 finely sliced blackcurrant leaves. Top with soda water and serve with a stirring rod (straw or spoon if not!). Garnish with the sprig of blackcurrant sage flowers and blackcurrant leaves. You could add a hollyhock flower, too.

FIELD OF DREAMS

This cocktail came about by happy accident, following a glut of peas. I wanted to represent a field bursting with meadow flowers: the green grass was easy to replicate with the peas.

4 mint leaves, preferably spearmint (Mentha spicata)
dash of Elderflower Liqueur (page 24)
I egg white
¾ oz (20 ml) Kamm & Sons apéritif
¾ oz (20 ml) floral gin, such as Jensen Old Tom
2 oz (60 ml) Pea Purée (see below)
2 tsp (10 ml) freshly squeezed lemon juice
edible flowers, such as oxeye daisies, cornflowers, wild vetch sprig, to garnish (do NOT eat more than one sprig of wild vetch, as they are toxic in large doses)

Smack the mint leaves between your palms and drop into a cocktail shaker. Add the Elderflower Liqueur and egg white. Cover the shaker and dry-shake hard for 20 seconds, then add the remaining ingredients and fill the shaker two-thirds of the way up with ice. Cover again and shake hard for another 20 seconds. Double-strain the mixture into a highball glass, using the tea strainer to catch any mint solids. Place your edible flowers on the foam and serve immediately.

PEA PURÉE

Mix ¼ cup (60 g) of fresh or thawed frozen small peas with just enough water to liquefy the peas in a blender. Pulse for a few seconds, then turn up to high for 15 seconds. Strain through a fine mesh to ensure that the purée is smooth.

PEAR AND LAVENDER HEAVEN

This is a floral delight for the taste buds and not bad to look at either. Lavender and pears work really well together. If you don't have pear purée, pear juice will work fine. And if you have no Meadowsweet Syrup, you could always use elderflower cordial or syrup.

4 basil leaves
½ oz (15 ml) Meadowsweet Syrup (page 22)
2 oz (60 ml) Lavender Gin (page 11)
1 oz (30 ml) organic pear purée
½ oz (15 ml) freshly squeezed lemon juice
lavender sprig, slice of lemon zest, to garnish

Chill a martini glass thoroughly in the freezer or refrigerator for 2 or 4 hours respectively. Alternatively, fill the glass with ice.

Smack the basil leaves between your palms to release the essential oils and drop into the cocktail shaker. Add the remaining ingredients. Fill a shaker two-thirds of the way up with ice, cover, and shake hard for 20 seconds. If you used ice to chill your glass, empty it out. Double-strain the cocktail into the chilled glass with the tea strainer. Garnish with the sprig of lavender and lemon zest.

THE CHERRY BLOSSOM

Japan is known for its cherry blossom celebrations—a very short season when this beautiful flower takes center stage—and even on London streets, the drama of cherry blossoms falling from the trees like confetti is not just a visual feast. The blossoms themselves can be candied for a wonderful garnish or dried and mixed with salt for a cocktail rim. I have used Japanese ingredients in this cocktail to bring a little of Japan to London.

¾ oz (20 ml) yuzu or lemon juice
dried pink cherry blossom, ground into pink salt
1 oz (30 ml) plum wine
1 oz (30 ml) vodka
½ oz (15 ml) sake
2 tsp (10 ml) sour cherry juice
candied pink cherry blossom (page 25), to garnish

Chill a martini glass thoroughly in the freezer or refrigerator for 2 or 4 hours respectively.

Dip the glass into a saucer of yuzu or lemon juice and then turn the outside edge of the glass into the salted cherry blossom mix. Pour the remaining ingredients into the cocktail shaker, fill it two-thirds of the way up with ice, and shake hard for 20 seconds. Strain the contents of the shaker into the chilled glass and garnish with a candied pink cherry blossom.

THE HONEYSUCKLE

The stunning honeysuckle (Lonicera periclymenum) blossoms appear in early summer and provide a heady scent around the garden at Midnight Apothecary. I have used some vodka here to maintain the strength of the cocktail but not drown out the taste of honeysuckle. The sweet, sharp mint opens up the palate to make the drink balanced and refreshing (see photo on page 2).

5 spearmint (*Mentha spicata*) leaves
1 oz (30 ml) cognac (or mid-range brandy)
½ oz (15 ml) vodka
¾ oz (20 ml) Honeysuckle Syrup (page 16)
¾ oz (20 ml) freshly squeezed lemon juice
honeysuckle blossom, to garnish

Chill a martini glass thoroughly in the freezer or refrigerator for 2 or 4 hours respectively. Alternatively, fill the glass with ice.

Smack the mint leaves between the palms of your hands to release the essential oils and drop them into the cocktail shaker. Add the cognac, vodka, Honeysuckle Syrup, and lemon juice. Fill the shaker two-thirds of the way up with ice, cover, and shake hard for 20 seconds. If you used ice to chill your glass, empty it out. Strain the cocktail into the chilled glass. Garnish with the honeysuckle blossom and serve.

RASPBERRY AND SCENTED GERANIUM SOUR

This very pretty, delicious, pink cocktail is a riff on raspberries and lemon treated in various ways, with an extra layer of depth provided by the use of scented geraniums and vinegar. Although you can't taste it directly, the vinegar in the Shrub gives a savory umami depth, which is rounded off with a dash of angostura bitters. The frothy body of the egg-white foam provides a mildness and beautiful mouth feel in contrast to the strong, punchy gold rum, creating a very balanced, luxurious cocktail.

1 oz (30 ml) Scented Geranium Vodka (page 11)

1 oz (30 ml) gold rum

¾ oz (20 ml) Lemon Verbena and Raspberry Syrup (page 23)

2 tsp (10 ml) Raspberry and Scented Geranium Shrub (page 9)

2 tsp (10 ml) freshly squeezed lemon juice

1 egg white

dash of angostura bitters

scented geranium (*Pelargonium*) leaf, 3 tiny edible flowers, such as rosemary or viper's bugloss (*Echium vulgare*), to garnish

Chill a martini glass thoroughly in the freezer or refrigerator for 2 or 4 hours respectively. Alternatively, fill the glass with ice.

Pour all the ingredients (but no ice) into a cocktail shaker. Cover and dry-shake hard for 20 seconds to consolidate all the ingredients and really emulsify the egg white. Add ice to the shaker, cover again, and shake hard for another 20 seconds. If you used ice to chill your glass, empty it out. Strain the cocktail into the chilled glass. Let the egg-white foam settle. Place the scented geranium leaf and the 3 edible flowers on top of the foam, using tweezers if necessary, and then serve.

LEMON BALM AND NASTURTIUM DAISY

Maybe there are a confusing number of flowers in this recipe name, but "daisy" refers purely to the style of cocktail (a type of sour). Here I have used a base of Nasturtium Gin, to which I've added a small amount of Lemon Balm Liqueur, plus a slug of orgeat syrup for that almond flavor.

2 oz (60 ml) Nasturtium Gin (page 14)
2 tsp (10 ml) Lemon Balm Liqueur (page 23)
½ oz (15 ml) orgeat syrup
½ oz (15 ml) freshly squeezed lemon juice
dash of soda water
lemon zest, lemon balm (*Melissa officinalis*) leaf,
nasturtium leaf, to garnish

Fill a rocks glass with ice. Combine all the ingredients, except the soda water and garnish, in a cocktail shaker. Fill it two-thirds of the way up with ice. Cover and shake hard for 20 seconds. Strain the mixture into the glass over the ice. Add the garnish, and top with a dash of soda water.

NASTURTIUM COLLINS

Throughout summer and into the fall, nasturtiums grow out of control in the garden at Midnight Apothecary, so I feel no guilt about harvesting huge amounts to keep a semblance of order. They not only look glorious but they also taste wonderful. Both the leaves and flowers have a pepperiness that works particularly well with rum and tequila. We use Nasturtium Rum made with golden rum, not just for its flavor but also for the dramatic amber color you get once it is diluted against the yellow, orange, and red flowers.

1½ oz (45 ml) Nasturtium Rum (page 14)
1 oz (30 ml) Ginger Syrup (page 16)
½ oz (15 ml) freshly squeezed lemon juice
4 oz (120 ml) soda water
nasturtium flowers, nasturtium leaves, to garnish

Fill a collins glass with ice. Pour the Nasturtium Rum, Ginger Syrup, and lemon juice into a cocktail shaker. Fill it two-thirds of the way up with ice, cover, and shake hard for 20 seconds. Strain the mixture into the glass over the ice. Top with the soda water, and garnish with the nasturtium flowers and leaves.

THE ELDER SOUR

The Elder Sour is a well-known cocktail—some people use vodka, others gin, and some just Elderflower Liqueur, which, in this case, is vodka-based. This is a pure celebration of the elderflower so we are keeping it simple, with lemon and lime juices providing the right balance of acidity to cut through the liqueur.

2 oz (60 ml) Elderflower Liqueur (page 24)
½ oz (15 ml) freshly squeezed lime juice
½ oz (15 ml) freshly squeezed lemon juice
I egg white
dash of orange bitters
sprig of elderflower blossom, to garnish

Chill a martini glass thoroughly in the freezer or refrigerator for 2 or 4 hours respectively, or fill the glass with ice. Add all the ingredients to a cocktail shaker, cover, and dry-shake hard for at least 20 seconds to emulsify the egg white. Fill the shaker two-thirds full with ice, cover, and shake hard for another 20 seconds. If you used ice to chill the glass, empty it out. Strain the contents of the shaker into the chilled glass. Garnish with elderflower blossom.

BLOODY ROSEMARY

This is an indulgent, colorful drink. It's on the sweet side, but the herbal notes of the rosemary in the essential oils, released by smacking a fresh sprig between your palms, as well as adding a small amount of rosemary syrup, together with the bitter notes of the peach bitters, redeem it. Bitter and sweet—that's love.

1 blood orange wheel

1 rosemary sprig

1 oz (30 ml) floral gin, such as Jensen Old Tom

1 oz (30 ml) blood orange liqueur, such as Solerno

2 tsp (10 ml) Rosemary Syrup (page 15)

½ oz (15 ml) freshly squeezed lemon juice

½ oz (15 ml) freshly squeezed blood orange juice

3 dashes of peach bitters

flowering rosemary sprig, to garnish

Place the blood orange wheel inside a rocks glass. Smack the rosemary sprig between your palms to release the essential oils and place in a cocktail shaker. Add the remaining ingredients, and fill the shaker two-thirds of the way up with ice. Cover and shake hard for 20 seconds. Fill the glass with ice. Double-strain the cocktail into the glass, using the tea strainer to catch the rosemary needles.

Garnish with the flowering rosemary sprig.

THE MIGHTY MEADOWSWEET

Meadowsweet is ridiculously delicious in a syrup, and its almond and honey notes come to the fore in this cocktail. The blossom appears at the height of summer, so this tastes of summer nights to me. The oranges in the Grand Marnier and the sweet, nutty, spicy, vanilla, and floral notes of an oak-barrel-aged brandy as fine as cognac are a perfect marriage with the meadowsweet.

1½ oz (45 ml) cognac
2 tsp (10 ml) Grand Marnier
½ oz (15 ml) Meadowsweet Syrup (page 22)
¾ oz (20 ml) freshly squeezed lemon juice
dash of orange bitters
small sprig of meadowsweet blossom, to garnish

Chill a martini glass thoroughly in the freezer or refrigerator for 2 or 4 hours respectively. Alternatively, fill the glass with ice.

Pour all the ingredients into a cocktail shaker. Fill the shaker two-thirds of the way up with ice. Cover and shake hard for 20 seconds. If you used ice to chill your glass, empty it out. Strain the contents of the shaker into the chilled glass. Garnish with a small sprig of (bug-free) meadowsweet blossom.

HEDGEROW SOUR

The color and texture, let alone exquisite taste, of this winter cocktail is a worthy prize for your foraging efforts. Rosehips, around from late summer into the winter, provide exotic floral elegance. Crab apples are transformed into a thick, pectin-rich, orangey-pink, appley, almost tropical syrup. The pressed juice of the raw crab apples in the Crab Apple Verjuice provides us with malic acid to balance the sweetness. The egg white tones down the strength and also the sweetness.

2 oz (60 ml) floral gin, such as Jensen Old Tom
¾ oz (20 ml) Crab Apple Verjuice (page 10) or freshly squeezed lemon juice
½ oz (15 ml) Crab Apple Syrup (page 20)
½ oz (15 ml) Rosehip Syrup (page 19)
1 egg white
candied rosehip (page 25), lemon spiral, toothpick (cocktail stick), to garnish

Chill a martini glass thoroughly in the freezer or refrigerator for 2 or 4 hours respectively. Alternatively, fill the glass with ice.

Add all the ingredients to a cocktail shaker, cover, and dry-shake hard for 30 seconds. Fill the shaker two-thirds of the way up with ice, cover again, and shake hard again for 20 seconds. If you used ice to chill your glass, empty it out. Strain the contents of the shaker into the chilled glass. Skewer the candied rosehip onto the toothpick (cocktail stick) and wrap the lemon spiral around it. Serve immediately.

WILD STRAWBERRY AND ROSE DAIQUIRI

Strawberries and roses are from the same family (Rosaceae) that gives us so much pleasure, from apples and pears to these two beauties. Wild strawberries (Fragraria vesca or F. virginiana) are those tiny, jewel-like treasures that you sometimes find in woodland clearings and meadows, on forest edges and along trails, and even in some quiet urban areas. Here they are combined with white rum and Rose Petal Syrup to conjure up summer meadows on a hot day.

1½ oz (45 ml) white rum
¾ oz (20 ml) Rose Petal Syrup (page 18)
2 tsp (10 ml) freshly squeezed lime juice
10 wild strawberries or 3 large strawberries, hulled and halved
⅔ cup (100 g) crushed ice
3 wild strawberries, toothpick (cocktail stick), to garnish

Combine all the ingredients in a blender and pulse/blend at a high speed for 30 seconds or until smooth. Pour into a rocks glass. Garnish with 3 wild strawberries on a toothpick (cocktail stick).

WILD VIOLET SOUR

This delicious spring cocktail should provide an extraordinary color. However, your Wild Violet Syrup may be quite pale and, in any case, it will turn pink when combined with lemon, so I suggest you add a couple of dashes of cassis to intensify the violet shade. If you do, add a couple more drops of lemon juice.

1½ oz (45 ml) dry gin
¾ oz (20 ml) Wild Violet Syrup (page 17)
½ oz (15 ml) freshly squeezed lemon juice
dash of crème de cassis or other
blackcurrant/blackberry liqueur (optional)
1 egg white
wild violet flower/candied wild violet flower, to garnish

Chill a martini glass thoroughly in the freezer or refrigerator for 2 or 4 hours respectively. Alternatively, fill the glass with ice.

Pour all the ingredients into a cocktail shaker. Cover and dry-shake hard for 20 seconds to emulsify the egg white. Fill the shaker two-thirds of the way up with ice, cover, and shake hard for another 20 seconds. If you used ice to chill the glass, empty it out. Strain the contents of the shaker into the chilled glass. Garnish with a fresh or candied wild violet flower.

BLACKBERRY AND LILAC COBBLER

I've been playing around with mezcal as its earthy smokiness fits the vibe of Midnight Apothecary metaphorically, although not always practically—it's a tricky ingredient to match. But in this case, it works with the lilac (Syringa vulgaris), blackberries, and Sloe Gin to provide a great little cocktail.

6 blackberries (save 1 for the garnish)
1 tsp (5 ml) blackcurrant cassis
1½ oz (45 ml) sloe gin
1 oz (30 ml) mezcal
½ oz (15 ml) freshly squeezed lemon juice
½ oz (15 ml) Lilac Syrup (page 19)
3 individual lilac blossoms, short straw, to garnish

Fill a rocks glass with crushed ice to just below the rim. Muddle 5 blackberries with the cassis in the bottom of the cocktail shaker. Add the other ingredients, cover, and shake hard, without ice, for 20 seconds. Strain the contents of the shaker over the crushed ice into the glass. Add the garnish of blackberry and lilac blossoms. Serve with a straw.

BERRIED TREASURE

This is essentially a French 77 cocktail, which uses Elderflower Liqueur to provide the sweetness, unlike the French 75, which uses simple syrup, in addition to gin, lemon juice, and champagne. I have no idea why it is called a French 77 when you use elderflower liqueur! This take on the French 75/77 garnish uses berry flavor pearls, available from online gourmet catering suppliers. These "bullets" of flavor are made from foraged fruit like blackberries, rose hips, crab apples, and sloes. I would recommend serving this drink with a long spoon, so that your guests can savor the tiny jewels in its hidden depths.

1 tsp berry flavor pearls
2 oz (60 ml) gin
½ oz (15 ml) Elderflower Liqueur (page 24)
1 oz (30 ml) freshly squeezed lemon juice
2 oz (60 ml) Champagne, prosecco, or other dry sparkling wine
lemon spiral, to garnish

Place the flavor pearls in the bottom of a champagne flute. Pour the gin, Elderflower Liqueur, and lemon juice into the cocktail shaker. Fill it two-thirds of the way up with ice. Cover and shake hard for 20 seconds. Strain the contents into the flute. Top up with Champagne or sparkling wine. Garnish with a lemon spiral and serve with a long spoon.

THE YARROW

The bittersweet taste of the tequila has been balanced by adjusting the ratios of ingredients in a classic Sour to two parts strong, one part sour, and half part sweet, and adding three dashes of bitters. It makes for a very refreshing cocktail.

2 oz (60 ml) Reposado tequila
½ oz (15 ml) Yarrow Syrup (page 20)
1 oz (30 ml) freshly squeezed lemon juice
3 dashes of cherry bitters
wild yarrow (*Achillea millefolium*) flower, to garnish

Chill a martini glass thoroughly in the freezer or refrigerator for 2 or 4 hours respectively. Alternatively, fill the glass with ice.

Add all the ingredients to a cocktail shaker. Fill it two-thirds of the way up with ice. Cover and shake hard for 10 seconds. If you used ice to chill your glass, empty it out. Strain the cocktail into the chilled glass, and garnish with a wild yarrow flower.

GORSE COLLINS

Gorse Flower Syrup has a beautiful but delicate almond and honey flavor, which I didn't want to overpower, but it does need a spirit with a complementary flavor, rather than a tasteless vodka, say, or the drink will be insipid.

1½ oz (45 ml) False Acacia Gin (page 12)
1 oz (30 ml) Gorse Flower Syrup (page 17)
½ oz (15 ml) freshly squeezed lemon juice
approx. 3 oz (90 ml) soda water (according to taste)
gorse blossoms, to garnish

Fill a collins glass with ice. Pour the False Acacia Gin, Gorse Flower Syrup, and lemon juice into the cocktail shaker. Fill two-thirds of the way up with ice. Cover, shake hard for 20 seconds, then strain the contents into the glass over the ice. Garnish with individual gorse blossoms and top with soda water.

INDEX